God, Mom, and Me

"A mother's messages from Heaven"

A true story about sharing love between a

mother and a daughter

-- and when life is done, death does not have the power to break

that bond.

by

Dian George

and

Co-Author and Illustrator Kevin Cress

Order this book online at www.trafford.com
or email orders@trafford.com

Most Trafford titles are also available at major online book retailers.

Print information available on the last page.

ISBN: 978-1-5539-5237-4 (sc)

Trafford rev. 06/26/2018

 www.trafford.com

North America & international
toll-free: 1 888 232 4444 (USA & Canada)
fax: 812 355 4082

This book is a tribute to my mother,
Marjorie A. Saunders.

She made a tremendous impression
on this world while she was here.

I also know that if anyone
could send messages from Heaven,
certainly it would be her.

ABOUT THE COVER

"The Fruit of the Spirit" tapestry was designed by Mason Bouvier, Inc., Ontario, Canada. The tapestry depicts the Holy Spirit descending as Christ was ascending to Heaven. It hangs in the sanctuary of Our Savior Lutheran Church located in Vero Beach, Florida. It was given by the author in honor of her mother, Marjorie A. Saunders, for all of our loved ones who have passed before us. It is hoped that each of us, during our journey through life, can be enriched by experiencing and practicing love, patience, self control, gentleness, faithfulness, goodness, kindness, and joy. If we can accomplish these things during our lifetime, then truly our souls have been blessed with the "Fruit of the Spirit."

This lovely key chain and bookmark depicting the
"Fruit of the Spirit" tapestry are available by request.

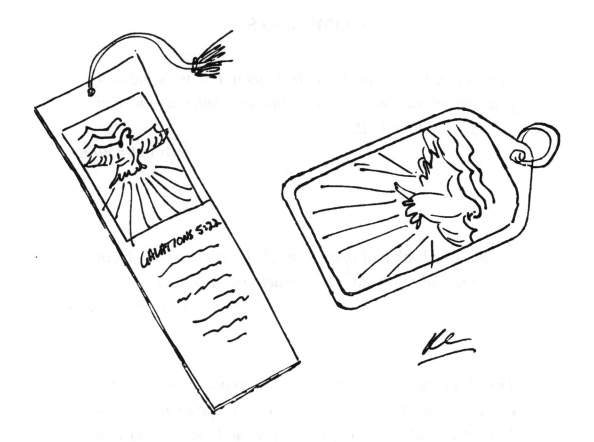

COMMENTS

You know, your book tells about your mother's life and your life interwoven with hers, and your spiritual journey -- Gee, that'll make it.

Sylvia Browne

I think this book will open people's hearts and give them empathy and understanding, which people often pass by.

Rosalie Cooney

This book makes a statement or reveals something for everyone -- humor, grief, deep sorrow, compassion, joy, and love. It reminds me of absolute truth and I was reminded of my mom's favorite passage of scripture, Corinthians 13:8, "Love never ends."

Pearl Stafura

ACKNOWLEDGMENTS

I wish to thank the following people for helping me make this book possible:

Sylvia Browne, who was there when I so desperately needed peace and comfort through her books, the Montel Williams show, and my personal reading. I'd like to also thank my friends and family who always offered me encouragement.

CONTENTS

INTRODUCTION

I took a deep breath and stepped into the SAS Shoe Store where my mother and I used to shop for shoes together. I hadn't been there in over two years and the memories were running rampant in my mind. Because Mother had suffered from Rheumatoid Arthritis, we felt very fortunate to be able to get shoes for her anywhere at all. SAS was the place that could fit her. We always enjoyed the free popcorn and nickel cokes they offered there. Now, over two years later, there were some changes -- my mother was not with me, the cokes cost a dime, and my shoes, which used to be $65 were $84.

I found my shoes, had some popcorn, and bought a coke. When it came to pay for my shoes, I shared with a congenial clerk, Madeline, that it had been over two years since my last visit.

"Does Marlene still work here?" I inquired.

"Yes, I'll tell her you were in."

And then I could not help but tell her that my mom and I always would come in together and that on February 20, 1999 (Saturday) she died. I explained that we loved coming in to get new shoes and how much fun we shared just being in the store. Madeline seemed very touched so I shared that, yes, I'm writing a book called *God, Mom and Me* and it is about how after my mother's death that nine or ten things occurred for which there is no explanation for except that my mother is trying to tell me that she is not far away. I gave Madeline an example regarding whether I could go on a cruise again alone since that is what my mom and I shared as being "Very Special" together. My uncle in Ohio had

called two weeks earlier and asked if I would join my aunt and him on a cruise to the Caribbean in February -- February 17th to be exact. I told them I would think it over and call them back the following day at 2:00 p.m. and tell them one way or the other if I would go.

That evening when I went to bed, my mother came to me in a dream.

My mother's bedroom is exactly the way it was when she left it. Her purse still sits on her desk and in it is her checkbook containing $70 in cash and $500 in her checking account. In my dream, my mother had her suitcase on her bed and she was packing.

I said to her, "Mother, may I speak to you because I haven't seen you in two years."

Her response was, "Not now, I'm packing, and you don't need to think you are leaving me here because I'm going along."

I called my uncle the next day and told him, of course, I'm going along on the cruise! The death of my mother is not only hard on me, but also on my Aunt Gerry, who is my mother's sister, and her husband, Jim, because they were very close and would visit us in our home in Florida for two weeks every February. They have done this for the past seventeen years. Last year I met them to relax and vacation at Dolphin Island in Alabama, which was the first anniversary of her death. This year, we will be on that cruise. Madeline found this fascinating and she was very touched by my story. I told her I lived 54 years without anything out of the ordinary happening to me -- and I shared one more thing with her -- about my mother always saving quarters to put in the slot machines on our cruises, which I will also share with you later on in this book. Madeline seemed quite

4

taken by this. The only thing anyone seemed to come up with is that my mother and I were so close, it seems that she isn't very far away.

Within these pages, I hope to share her life, my life interwoven, and my spiritual journey.

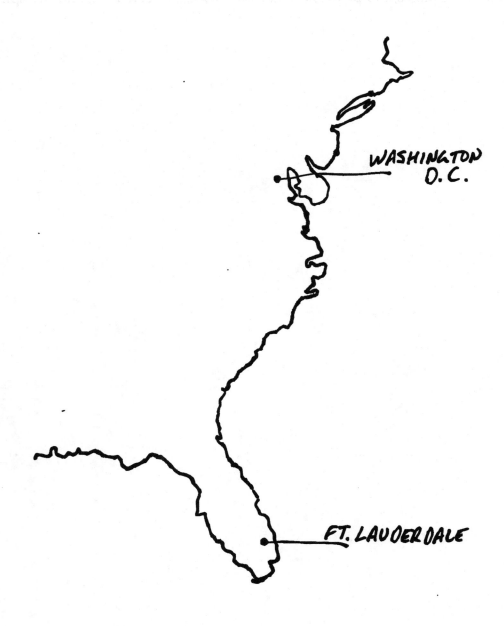

WASHINGTON
D.C.

FT. LAUDERDALE

I. GETTING TOGETHER

Washington, D.C. is a place to experience and everyone should have the opportunity to live there. For me, a Marine, I was stationed in Quantico, Virginia, and lived in Temple Hills, Maryland, which is located eight miles from the White House. The traffic-congested commute over the Wilson Bridge twice a day provides enough headache material to write an entire book in itself. In fact, I always said I could read *War and Peace* (the longest book ever written) twice while waiting to get over the bridge.

I had been in the Marine Corps since 1971 and in 1982, I found myself stationed at Quantico, Virginia, commuting from Maryland.

My situation had developed along with my mother's at two opposite ends of the East Coast. We were each alone and since she was in Ft. Lauderdale, Florida, and I was in Maryland, we decided to join forces and live togther in Maryland.

She sold her home in Ft. Lauderdale and in 1982 we began living together and sharing a household. I cannot imagine a more joyous time. She played Mahjong at Andrews Air Force Base with the officer's wives and I enjoyed commuting to Quantico, just being a Marine. This may seem a bit over simplified, but as I look back, we were extremely contented during this period of time.

She seemed to be very happy and she enjoyed what she was doing and for the first time in a long time, she didn't need to work. I didn't know that people could be so

happy, but everything was so good -- looking back, it is hard to imagine that life could have such few troubles.

I used to carry a little blue lunch bag, and since Mother wasn't working, she enjoyed packing a lunch for me to take to work. Often times I would find little notes with happy faces on them in my lunch bag and they would say, "Have a good day." It's kind of ironic thinking of a forty-one-year-old woman Marine officer having her lunch packed by her mother with the bag containing "Happy Faces." Oh well, they always say Marines have soft hearts. They might also say, "So do their mothers."

Commuting to Quantico and having my mother as my dependent ended in November 1985 when I experienced being passed over for promotion to Major and it was time for me to leave the United States Marine Corps. There were lots of reasons for this, which belongs in another book, but the important thing here is the support and understanding that was provided by my mother, who always stood by my side as my Marine Corps career was coming to an end.

My mother never showed disappointment that my career was ending. I always thought she was just showing a stiff upper lip to keep my spirits up and really deep down she was hurting over this. But, to my amazement, she really wasn't disappointed that my career was ending. I found out a lot of things the day Sylvia Browne tuned into my life. This was just one of them. I want to share this because of the enlightening message I was given. I was told that she's glad I'm out of it because she always worried

11

-- as a mother, but she was excessively worried. She was always afraid that I would get

blown up, hurt, or shot. So now I know, she was happy I would no longer be serving

my country and she didn't have to worry about this any more.

II. MOVING FROM MARYLAND

The move from Maryland was both filled with anticipation and also reluctance. The anticipation was to start a new life and new way of doing things. The reluctance set in due to leaving my cat, Geraldine, who had died about a year ago. She had been placed in a sealed container and buried in the front yard of the Temple Hills, Maryland home.

In fact, I resolved myself that I just couldn't leave her. I had this terrible impression in my mind that the neighborhood would decline and Geraldine was left in the front yard. I just couldn't do it. I put this on the back burner and decided to deal with it later -- after all, at this point we had no place to go.

The decision of where we go from here was up for discussion and all avenues were open. We kind of tuned into Florida because we like it there, but really weren't resolved to return to Ft. Lauderdale since it had become crowded and crime-ridden. We considered throwing a dart on the map of the United States and going where it landed. Then Mother discussed how she and my stepfather, Tom, had considered a little town called Vero Beach, and how he always wanted to visit a place called Village Green. He had seen it in a magazine and thought that it would be a very nice place to live. Also, my mother recalled our former neighbors in Ohio were now living in Vero Beach. She had known them for 40 years. We felt it would be very nice to be in the same town with them again. She called them to let them know we were considering locating in Vero Beach and she asked them why they liked it. They explained that they go shrimping off the Wabasso Bridge and shrimp cocktail is very plentiful at no cost. This kind of sealed the plans to

14

15

head for Vero Beach, Florida and make this our new address.

We knew November 8, 1985 would be the last day I would serve actively in the United States Marine Corps, so in October we opted for me to take leave and for us to go to Vero Beach to look for a place to live.

I took ten days leave; we drove to Vero Beach and while there stayed with our friends of 40 years and located a home for us to begin a new chapter in our lives. While we were there, my sister, Chris, and her boyfriend met with us and decided to also make the move from Ft. Lauderdale to Vero Beach. In their preparations to make the move, my mother and I joined them in Ft. Lauderdale for a couple of days. When we all arrived there, my mother and I stayed at my sister's apartment. The following incident confirmed the decision for my sister's move to Vero Beach: As we were settling in and relaxing from the drive from Vero Beach, my sister decided to empty the trash which would be picked up the next day. She went downstairs to the dumpster and noticed two men fooling around her vehicle. They told her they were repossessing the vehicle which was a 1978 Mercury Bob Cat. She asked them why they were removing the hatchback if they were repossessing it. They said they weren't taking it off -- they were trying to put it back on because "Carman," the owner of the car, said it was ready to fall off. Just then I had come out to check on my sister because she had been gone too long to just empty the trash. At that moment she informed them that the car belonged to her and that it had been paid for a long time and that there was nothing wrong with the hatchback and there is no "Carman." I told her to call the police and I told the men to just stand by and we'll get this

straightened out. They made no attempt to leave and in a few minutes a squad car pulled up. The policeman checked the men out. They had a clipboard and on it was a long list of car parts among which was a '78 Ford or Mercury hatchback. It almost seemed as if the police were in on it because the men didn't seem worried, they didn't run and the policeman let them go, reporting to us that they just had the wrong car they were trying to repossess. After that, we all decided that a hundred or so miles up the road would be good for all of us.

III.   MAKING THE MOVE

November 8, 1985 came sooner than we expected. The moving van had come and everything was loaded and it headed for Vero Beach.

Our car was loaded. My mother had her dachshund, Heidi; I had my dog, Blondie, Geraldine's daughter, Geraldine, who was my Siamese cat, and my ferret, Beanie. And then my mother asked, "What are you doing with that shovel?" Geraldine was going with us. With that, all seven of us headed down the highway. Mother was not particularly pleased that I had dug Geraldine up and brought her with us. I assured her Geraldine smelled better dead than Heidi does alive.

We arrived in Vero Beach anticipating our new home. It was about noon on the 10th of November when we pulled into the ERA office to pick up the house key. As I was getting out of the car, someone came to the front door of the office and said, "Dian, you have a phone call." I couldn't imagine who would be calling me when I just arrived. I went into the office and answered the phone. I will never forget the words coming from the other end of the line. "Dian, your home loan has been canceled. I called back to Quantico, Virginia, and some sergeant told me you were no longer in the Marine Corps."

You can only imagine what I felt like returning to the car to tell my mother we had no place to go. Just like the trooper she always was, she said we will get through this, too. So with my mother, her dog Heidi, myself, my dog Blondie, Geraldine's daughter Geraldine, my ferret Beanie, and Geraldine in the sealed container, we had no place to go. To make matters worse, the moving van would arrive the next day to deliver our furniture

to the house that had just been taken away from us. Well, here we come -- I felt we were about to lose our friends of more than 40 years. But we were welcomed with open arms. It was now about 1:00 p.m. We unloaded our live cargo and I headed straight for the newspaper to look for rental houses. I promised our friends I would find a place for us before sundown because our furniture is due in the next day! I called a few prospects before I found someone that could possibly help us.

I called a man by the name of Cliff Reuter and he was the only one who seemed willing to help. I told him I needed an address before sundown and he seemed up to the challenge. He told me to meet him right away and he would show me what he had and we could make our choice. I left immediately and met him. He had a small home for rent and offered a warehouse for the overflow. Then he showed me a very satisfactory rental home. It was brand new. I told him I would return with my mother to approve the move. I also told him the other home was too small and entirely inadequate.

I returned with my mother and she was very satisfied. She reached in her purse for her checkbook and remembered she had left it back where we had been staying. So I said I would go get it and would return in a short while. While I was gone, Mr. Reuter pulled a switch-er-rooh and he told her the owner of the house would not permit our pets, but the little house would be fine. He talked her into the small one with a promise of a free warehouse for six months. I returned and she had such a big smile on her face, I didn't have the heart to cause a problem. It turned out that both houses belonged to Mr. Reuter and he had no intention of renting us the nice one.

The moving company was contacted with the new address and the moving truck arrived the next day, unloading what would fit in the small house and unloading the rest in the warehouse.

About the most challenging event to take place after our move took place when I was looking for employment and I applied to the Sheriff's office to be a road patrolman. They needed my birth certificate. And you've probably guessed right. The warehouse was filled top to bottom -- and I found my birth certificate in the bottom box at the far right back of the warehouse.

We looked for a permanent residence and as all things happen for a reason, we were able to find our perfect home and we moved in February 1986.

As it was, my mother and I shared 13 years of perfect harmony and good times and I was never happier in my life. We lived in a small town, went everywhere together, and I always felt I could never have shared my time with anyone else other than her. Life was good. Life was perfect. And I thought it always would be.

IV.   GOD/DOG

I am so appreciative that we returned to the church in 1998 after so many years. But as I look back, I can see the pattern of the phrase, "Everything happens for a reason." How did returning to the church play a part in this? The pieces of the puzzle all fit together. I had always felt that my mother and I certainly believed in God and it would be nice to belong to a church. It did cross my mind that if something happened to either one of us, the other one would have to find a pastor who would pretend to know us to give a Christian burial. But, what the heck, Mom says she will live to be a hundred so there is no need to rush and if I went first, well that's something that doesn't need taken care of at this point. What did God have in mind? Hindsight is always 20/20 and it really makes me smile when I think about how things developed. Today, I can clearly see how our lives progressed as if to be a scripted play.

Ironically, one day in October 1997, my mother told me to go to the Humane Society and bring home one of those dogs that were rescued from the Island of Montserrat after the volcano had erupted. She had been watching television and she watched how after all of the people had been evacuated from the island -- they just left the animals. A very kind man brought his boat in and rescued as many as he could catch. Eleven dogs were brought to the Vero Beach Humane Society for socialization and adoption. So, I was off on a mission. Which of the eleven would come home with me? Two of the dogs were presented to me, but I was immediately aware that these dogs needed a one-on-one tender, loving, 100% devotion to bring them back from the "hell" they encountered in the

aftermath of the volcano. Their pads were burnt from the intense heat created from the lava flow. There was no way I could bring one of these dogs into an environment where three other dogs were already king of the roost. So disappointed, I headed for the door to return home. On the way out, I noticed a blonde dog tied to the assistant director's chair. I asked about the dog and I was told that someone had been shown the dog, but they felt she had a funny look in her eye and they didn't want to take her home. Okay, the door was open – I already had permission to bring another dog home. I checked her out, brought her home, and my mother said, "She is a Suzie." I was happy and thought, "Isn't that just okay." This dog is named for the assistant director of the Humane Society, "Suzie" for short, or "Suzanne" to be formal. This dog had been spayed, which is always done when you get a dog from the Humane Society. I remember taking her to the vet and getting her checked out. She was just fine. I asked the doctor, "Don't her titties seem to be quite large?" She said, "They sure do."

On November 16, 1997 at 2:30 a.m. something woke me up. Suzie was with me. It was dark. The left side of my nightgown felt warm and wet. I heard a noise. What was that? I heard it again. It sounded like a little bark. I reluctantly, slowly, reached down my left side – it was warm and wet and smaller than my hand and moving. I brought it in front of the covers and exclaimed, "I have a puppy!!" My mother heard me from her room and I distinctly remember her saying, "You are getting shipped off to the VA!" "No, no, I really have a puppy." She said, "Okay, just remember, they never come in ones." She rolled over and went back to sleep. Meanwhile, I turned my light on, left the puppy in bed

with Suzie and I went to the kitchen for some warm milk. I sat on the patio and then checked on Suzie. There were now two. More warm milk. I checked again. There were three. More milk – there were four. More milk – there were five. They finally stopped. The following morning was Sunday and at 8:00 a.m. I called the executive director of the Humane Society to tell her Suzie was the proud mother of five puppies. She said she would get Susan and they would be right over. They arrived and got me all straightened around. We made a bed for them in my bedroom and for the next eight weeks, Suzie and I would take care of her beautiful puppies. They were named Suzie, Joan, Michael, Ernie, and Brenda, after our friends at the Humane Society and our veterinarians. I became especially attached to Ernie and desperately wanted to keep him.

The Humane Society was very helpful and promised me they would help me find homes for them when they were ready to leave their mother. The day came. We were to depart for our cruise on January 8, 1998 so the puppies needed to go to the Humane Society on January 7th. I removed the puppies as my mother expressed her wishes, "No, Ernie cannot stay. He must go, too." It was not easy to leave those adorable little ones. They were checked in and I cried. When I returned home, my uncle told me Suzie was in the puppy bed crying because her babies were gone.

The next morning we were off on our cruise. It was a ten-day cruise. By day five I had told my mother a hundred times that I am really going to miss Ernie and I wish I could have kept one of the pups. She finally relented and said I could have Ernie. We were in our room and I picked up the phone. We were in Cartagena, Colombia, and ship-

SHIP TO SHORE

to-shore is $45.00 a minute. I reached the Humane Society and Barbara answered the phone. I told her who I was and blurted out, "Mom says I can have Ernie!" Barbara said, "No you can't. Ernie's been adopted and by some really wonderful people." I looked down dejected and gave the news to mother. The little red head in her very authoritative manner responded back, "Well, they can just unadopt him." I told Barbara what she said and Barbara said, "Oh, no we can't."

After the cruise, I spoke with Joan, the director of the Humane Society. The puppies had all been adopted. "But Dian, we can have a puppy reunion," Joan offered. "We can have it in the day room." What a wonderful gesture. "That way you will get a chance to meet all of the puppies' new owners." "Oh, Joan, that would be so wonderful," I said. I could just envision a wonderful get together. Joan said she would present birth certificates to the puppies' parents at the reunion. We set a date and I began making preparations for a catered buffet. I made photo albums and provided each of the new owners a pictorial progression of their puppy from day one. On each photo album I placed a miniature rose. The girls received pink roses; the boys received blue roses.

The day finally arrived; the puppy reunion took place. We all had a wonderful time and I met all of the new owners. One in particular, I definitely had to meet. "Ernie's new owners!" "Hello, I'm Suzie's mom. I understand you have Ernie." And as Pastor Diane recounts the story, apparently I said, "And just what is it that you do?" I guess she could tell I wasn't exuberant over the idea that he had a new mother. Her response was, "I am the pastor of Our Savior Lutheran Church." I said, "Oh, my mother and I want to return

to church and we are Lutherans." That's all it took. She gave me her card and invited us to attend services. We did. We found a wonderful, caring environment and something to which we wanted to become involved. We joined the church on May 23, 1998.

Ernie's new name is Cosmo, and Pastor Diane and her husband Dennis call him the "Little Evangelist."

The stage was being set for what was yet to come.

WHEN GOD CREATED DOG

When God had made the earth and sky, the flowers and the trees, He then made all the animals, the fish, the birds and bees, and when at last He'd finished not one was quite the same.

He said I'll walk this world of mine and give each one a name and so he traveled far and wide and everywhere he went a little creature followed him until its strength was spent. When all were named upon the earth and in the sky and sea the little creature said, "Dear Lord, there's no name left for me." Kindly, the Father said to him:

"I've left you to the end,

I've turned my own name back to front

and called you DOG,

my friend.

Author unknown

Suzie and her puppies.

Pastor Diane and her husband Dennis
with Ernie (Cosmo) at the Puppy Party.

V.   OUR LIFE TOGETHER

Mother had two husbands. My father died at age 32 of cancer when I was 11. She married my stepfather when I was 12 and he died in Washington, D.C. in 1984. We brought him to Washington, D.C. to be close to us, but he was very sick and only stayed in our home two days and was hospitalized for over a year, and then passed away. She visited him every day and he wouldn't eat unless she was with him. She was very good to him and then he died. Then it was just the two of us.

As I look back, I don't know how hard it was for her. As long as I had her, I was strong. I believed there was nothing that we couldn't do. And she could have anything she wanted.

I would always remember my friend, Sandy Hookilou. She was also a Marine and she brought her mother to Woodbridge, Virginia to live with her. It had only been two or three months that her mother had lived with her and one day when Sandy came home from work, there was an ambulance in front of her house. Sandy was stricken with fear. She went into her house to find that her mother had died of a heart attack. I never did forget that and I vowed as long as I have my mother, she will have everything I can give her and I promised to love her every day and thank God that I am so fortunate to have her. Every day is a blessing.

I didn't know at the time we moved into our home in Vero Beach that I would only be allowed to be with her for 13 years.

During that time we worked hard, played hard, and I always kept my promise to

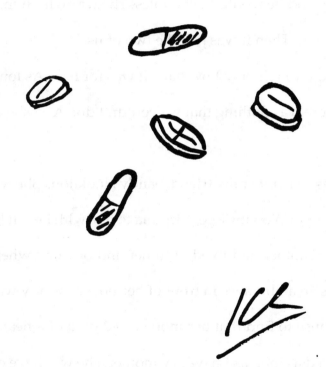

cherish her every day.

We went on cruises. She loved to dress up, go to captains' parties, and she was elegant -- a lady in all respects. She worked very hard and she earned the time that we spent on cruises.

And then on the 26th day of December 1996, we had just returned from a Caribbean cruise and she became ill. She went to Dr. Roseman and he removed an abscess. I took her home and she became worse. I called Dr. Roseman and he said something else is going on and that I better call 911. I did and she was hospitalized. Then came the news of "how long has she been diabetic?" I told them they have the wrong patient. I was told by the doctor that she may not have been a diabetic yesterday, but she is today. Two years later, the same doctor would tell me her heart stopped.

We got her all straightened around and the hospital gave us instructions and glucose strips and a glucose monitor to take home with us to combat this awful disease, sugar diabetes. And then sometime during the night, before she went home, someone came into her hospital room and stole her supplies. Both of us were new to this and the devastation was indescribable. I raised the roof and I'm sure it shook the whole hospital. Her supplies were replaced and she was discharged to begin a new chapter in her life of how to deal with Rheumatoid Arthritis and be a diabetic. She was taking prednisone for pain and insulin for her diabetes, which made her a very brittle diabetic. Little did either one of us know is that this was a death sentence.

For the next two years I watched my mother deteriorate. She always said that if this

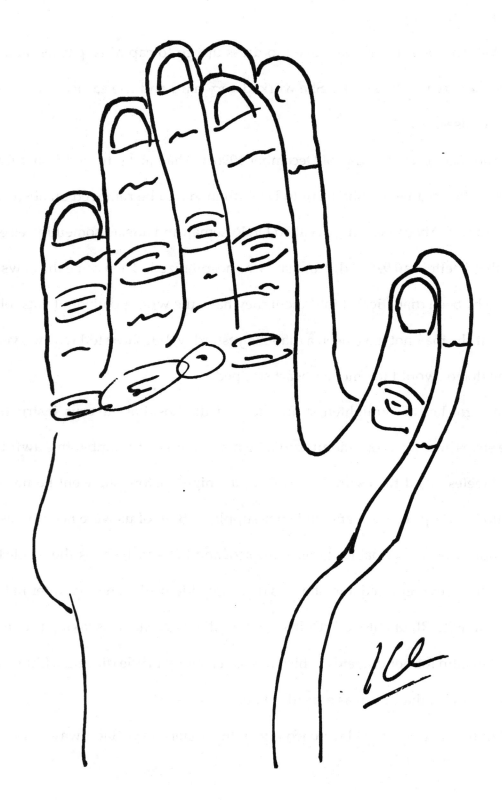

41

is what it takes to live, then she'd deal with it. I can honestly say she was probably more of a Marine than I was, she was certainly not willing to give up.

We came back from our cruise on December 13, 1998. She was not doing well, but she was hanging in there, just like always. I was just so frustrated. I said to her, "You never feel good any more." She said she would put herself in a nursing home. I said, "No, I didn't mean it that way, I just couldn't fix it." And that was so much unlike us. I guess neither of us knew what to do.

And then it came. On February 15, 1999 at 7:00 a.m. in the morning she asked me to get her new little dog, Ilsa, and put her out because she was in the bathroom with her bothering her. I put Ilsa out and I heard my mother holler, "Dian, nitro." I ran to her bedroom -- she came out of the bathroom and fell on her bed. I grabbed her purse and turned it inside out looking for the nitro glycerin. She had placed the small bottle in a larger pill container and I was in no shape to try to locate it. It was terrible. I grabbed the phone and called 911 -- it took forever for them to get to us. In the meantime, I found the nitro and I was trying to put it on top of her tongue all the while she was trying to get it under her tongue. They quietly carried her out. That was the last time she would be home. That was Monday. She was in intensive care and the doctors said there was nothing they could do to help her. But, in my mind, I said they don't know who they are dealing with -- she is in God's hands now. Her heart doctor said at one point he was pleasantly optimistic. But it was after that I was told there is nothing more that they can do. I said in that case, let me take her home to die. They told me she said, "No."

"EMERGENCY"

Saturday morning came and at 10:00 a.m. they were supposed to come and install new carpet in our home. I had gone to the hospital early so I could be home for the installers. At 9:00 a.m. Mother sat up and said, "I love you girls." I said, "And we love you, too." She said she would like her back rubbed, so I did. After a few minutes I came around to the other side of the bed to sit and hold her hand and to talk to her. Just then she said she had a pain in her throat and I ran and got the nurse. The nurse asked my mother on a scale of one to ten, ten like having a baby, what is your pain? Mother said a ten. The nurse made me go out of the room. I went to the ICU waiting room. There I heard them call "code blue ICU." I knew it was Mom. Then they came in -- the same doctor who had told me two years ago that my mother has diabetes -- now said, "Her heart stopped." They said she passed away at 9:18 a.m. I've always thought no, it was 9:15 a.m. My world stopped. They asked if I wanted to see her and I said, "No, not like that."

I went home and on the way I was stopped at the traffic light to make a left turn. I began to realize my mom died. Time has stood still since then.

God has a tendency to make you numb and you go through the motions. Funeral arrangements were done. It was in God's hands and leaving it up to Him, He took care of everything. Everything was perfect. I have never seen such a beautiful funeral. She wanted to be buried by a palm tree. Without us ever realizing it, she was placed in a crypt not 20 feet from a palm tree. Things just fell into place. There was a viewing at the funeral home, services at the church, and then a service at Hillcrest Memorial Gardens before she was placed in the crypt. This in itself would not be significant except later the events

SEMPER FI

Ke

45

would be identified in a reading by Sylvia Browne.

The funeral party gathered by her beautiful two-tone dark blue casket which had gold crosses at each of the four corners. The pastor did a beautiful memorial service and then champagne glasses were distributed to the guests. My sister gave everyone champagne and then she asked me to do a toast to my mother. Of course, the only appropriate toast would be "Semper Fi, Mom." At that moment, I knew my mom was more of a Marine than I'll ever be.

Those moments closed and then life began to seem to be so much less than it used to be. How can this world be so lonely at the loss of one person? It's not hard if that person is your whole life.

I needed to read. I needed to go to church. I began to put my whole heart and soul into helping people -- helping people will take my mind off of me and thinking about others is all I have left.

One day, shortly after my mother passed away, my friend and her sister were sitting on the patio waiting for me to come home. I was supposed to meet them at 3:00 p.m. They have a key to my home so they let themselves in and they were sitting on the patio. While sitting on the patio, the screen door opened as if someone had walked in and then it closed. My friends did not tell me about this until a long time later. My friends' sister and my mother did not always get along well together and they took this to be an omen that my mother did not appreciate her presence in our home. Whatever it was, they both said there was no breeze and the door had been latched. This was a strange

phenomenon that they chose not to share with me that day, but they kept it in mind for future reference. In the meantime, I began to experience my own strange phenomena.

VI.   THE QUARTER

The first strange event happened to me one day as I was doing my laundry. I took my yellow sheets out of the dryer and put them back on my bed. I stretched those sheets tight and then left the room. I remembered the bedspread that I wanted to wash and I went back to my room to get it. I entered the room and, lo and behold, there was a quarter dead center in the middle of my bed, laying on the top yellow sheet. There is no way that was there when I left the room. How in the world? I had no change when I made the bed. There is just no way to explain that.

After that, I was watching "Beyond Chance" one night on television. They began a segment that explained how a little boy was abducted from his home and he had been found murdered. His mother could not bear to pass through the door where her son had been removed from her home. One day, she left her home to do some errands and she reached into the console of her car to get her sunglasses. As the console door lifted up, she found that her glasses were not there. She returned to the house to get her glasses and when she got back to the car she found two pennies laying on the console. She, like I, knew they weren't there before because she had opened the lid and there was no way pennies could remain on the lid when it was being opened. Later, she also found two pennies in the threshold of the doorway. She felt her son was telling her that he is okay. It was explained that her son at age seven saved pennies and he had jars of them. Just as my mother saved quarters to put in slot machines, one appeared on my yellow sheets that day. After seeing the episode of "Beyond Chance," I began to sense something was also happening to me.

VII.   THE GREEN PAMPHLET

I had canceled the carpet installers the day my mother passed away and I made arrangements that sometime in the future I would contact them to replace carpet. The time finally came that I felt I probably would feel better getting it done, so I called them and arranged a new date for them to complete the job. I also called the waterbed store so the waterbeds could be disassembled while the other men were laying carpet.

The waterbed men had disassembled the beds and I was about to pay them for their services, but I wanted to check my bank balance before writing checks. I had a green glossy pamphlet in my hand and I told the men I would pay them, but I needed to make a phone call first. We had all been standing in the dining room and I had the green pamphlet in my hand. As I reached for the pamphlet, it was no longer in my hand. I asked them if they had seen what I had done with it and they said, "No." We all looked around the dining room and certainly the most obvious place for it to be would be the dining room table. No, it was not there. I told them I would need to find the green pamphlet first and then call the bank and then I would pay them. We were all leaving the dining room -- I was the last to leave and on my way out I heard something slap on the carpet. I turned and there was the green pamphlet, laying on the carpet. It was too far from the dining room table to have fallen off of it. Uh oh. Now, what was going on here? More strange phenomena -- was mother trying to tell me that she was here with me? Oh well, whatever it is -- it is pretty strange stuff.

At this time, I was trying to figure out my life. I began to attend church regularly

"Sylvia"

and again I set my goals to help as many people as I could -- just to retain my sanity. I read everything spiritual that I could get my hands on.

It was at this time that I happened to turn on the Montel Williams show and Sylvia Browne was appearing. It was the first time I had seen her and I was very impressed by the way she seemed to be so gifted and could tune into people's lives. I had never seen anything like that before.

I went to the bookstore and bought as many of Sylvia Browne's books that I could find on the shelf. One in particular, *The Other Side and Back*, had in the back of it where Sylvia Browne's office could be contacted. I called the number and I was able to speak with Michael, Sylvia Browne's secretary. I told him I was very much interested in having Sylvia do a reading for me. I found out very quickly that she is booked two years in advance and that my reading was scheduled for January 23, 2002 at 4:00 p.m. on a Wednesday. Oh my, I am really scheduled. What could she possibly tell me and is she really psychic or do they check you out in advance and know all about you before the reading? After all, they have two years to work on it.

VIII. Mom, I Need a Sign So Bad

Some time had passed and adjusting to not having my best friend was not coming easily. My friend Marge was very close to my mother and she was also having a hard time dealing with her absence.

One evening my friend was visiting with me and she brought her dog with her. His name was Bumper.

I was having a very bad "miss Mom" moment and I excused myself because I felt I needed to be alone for a few minutes. About the only place to be alone would be in the bathroom. I sat down on the only available seat and proceeded to bawl my eyes out. Tears were flowing down my cheeks and I was saying to myself, "Please, Mom, just give me a sign. I need a sign so bad. I miss you so much and I need something from you just so that I can go on." At that moment, my friend knocked on the bathroom door. I was surprised at the knock. I wiped my eyes and said, "Yes?" My friend asked if she could open the door. Again I said, "yes." She opened the door slightly and I noticed she had a strange look on her face. It seems that Bumper had gotten into the laundry basket and had taken his prey back behind the overstuffed chair in the corner of the family room. She knew how nasty Bumper could be when he had "prey" so she decided to use Mother's can grabber to retrieve it. She was successful in capturing the item and while it was hanging at the end of the can grabber, she returned it to the laundry basket. As she was passing through the kitchen to the laundry room, she felt my mother tap her on the shoulder and urge her to tell me quietly about what had just happened. She felt compelled to knock on the bathroom door and then she told me how my mother had come to her.

I said, "You're kidding." Once again, something occurred that was phenomenal. Am I imagining this or is it really happening? My thoughts were all jumbled and I was astounded. Am I bordering on being nuts and if I am, it is not only me, but it's happening to my friends, too.

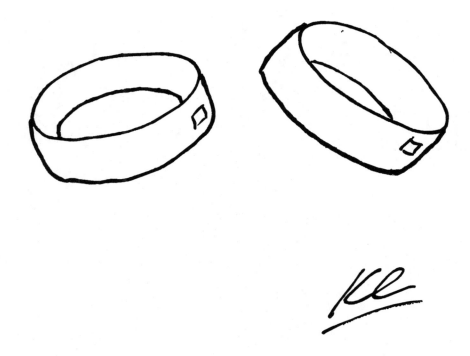

IX.   THE SILVER RINGS

This occurrence was within a few days after my mother's death. The funeral service was over. The impact of my loss was not yet registering, but there were still things that needed to be done. One of the hardest things to do was to invite family and friends into my mother's bedroom and ask them to find something of hers that they would like to take with them as a memento of my mother. Most everyone wanted a piece of her jewelry to remember her. Five or six people were invited to do this. My friend Marge was particularly interested in her silver rings that we had brought back from Cozumel, Mexico.

But, very strangely -- none of us could locate my mother's silver rings. All of us took turns going through her jewelry. They were not there.

After everyone made their selections, I was satisfied that I had done the right thing. My Aunt Gerry received her watch, which I had given to my mother for her birthday. It was purchased in St. Thomas and it was a beautiful gold watch with a mother of pearl face.

My sister chose her gold chains that she always admired and Mother's granddaughter chose her other watch and a few pieces of jewelry.

After everyone had taken what they wanted, I would continue searching the room for those silver rings. They were just not there -- not anywhere -- and it remained that way for almost a year.

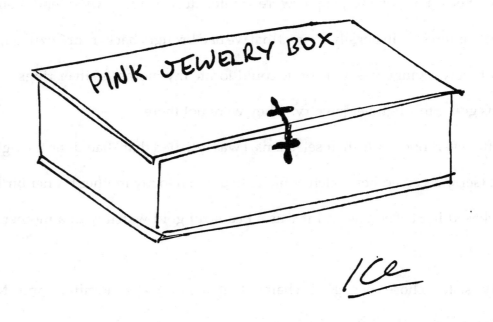

X.   THE PINK JEWELRY BOX

Usually the door of my mother's bedroom was closed. I would go in on occasion just to feel close to my mother. But as time passed, the occasions would be less frequent and certainly not an everyday basis.

One day, it occurred to me that there have to be more checks for the checking account of the rental house. They have to be in my mother's bedroom. I opened the door of her room to begin the search. It did not take long. My mother was always a neat-nik and everything had its place. That's why it was so strange about her missing silver rings. I opened her closet doors and at eye level of the center shelves, I noticed a box of checks. I picked up the box and opened it. There was the next book of checks in proper number sequence. I put the box of checks back where I had found them and I felt fortunate that they had been so easy to find. This may seem insignificant, but certainly it will be an intriguing point in a few moments.

One day, almost a year to the day of my mother's death, I received a disturbing message in the mail regarding home insurance. I believe it was "Failure to pay premium due." This drove me to my mother's room and immediately to her closet where all of the important house papers were kept. The insurance papers were on a shelf to the left of the center shelves. My eyes and my attention were completely on finding the house insurance. Whoa! What is that on the center shelf at eye level, right in front of my face? Well, what do you know? A pink jewelry box. This is not possible. I removed the pink jewelry box, noting that it was sitting on top of the box of checks. As I opened it, I saw my mother's silver rings.

As it turned out, there was no problem with the insurance or the premium payment, but the impact of finding the pink jewelry box and the silver rings is beyond comprehension, especially since the box was found sitting on top of the box of checks. There is just no explanation. As far as someone else putting it there, I live alone.

An even more astounding revelation is that on February 28, 2002, Sylvia Browne asked me a question, "What about the rings?" Immediately I replied, "Oh yes, my mother took her silver rings and then about a year to the day, she put them back." Sylvia was not the least bit surprised. In fact, she confirmed that this is what they call "aport" in her line of work. And me? Well, at this point, all I could say is, "I know it." Absolutely in awe. First, about the incredible situation of finding the jewelry box and the silver rings after they had gone "missing" and then Sylvia Browne identifying them in her reading.

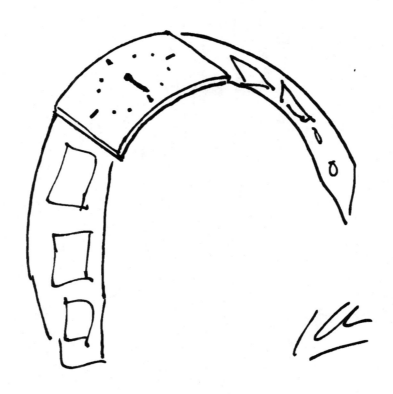

XI. THE WATCH

My watch said 3:15 p.m. I was busy studying at the last minute for my Bible Study assignment. I really felt that I was getting a lot done. Then the phone rang. It was Winnie, one of the ladies that I had promised to take with me to class. She said, "Dian, where are you?" "Why Winnie," as I looked at my watch, "It's only 3:15 and class is not until 6:00." Winnie said, "Dian, it's quarter to six!" I looked at my watch again and said, "Well, my watch has stopped, I'll be right there." I quickly grabbed my books and ran out the door and headed down the highway to pick up Winnie and Hope, desperately trying not to be late.

On our way to class, I was explaining to them that my watch stopped working and if Winnie hadn't called, I probably would have missed class. When we arrived, I noticed the pastor was aware that we had come in. On my way to my seat, I apologized to the pastor for being late and showed her that my watch had stopped. At that exact moment, the second hand on my watch began going around.

I was quite taken by that since my watch is battery operated. The amazing thing about it is that I am still wearing the same watch. It keeps perfect time and the battery has never been changed.

I have noted that this happened, identified it as being strange, and question how it can be explained. Did Mother do this? Is she trying to tell me that she is never far away? I have since found out that "they" are capable of making phones ring, dropping coins, and stopping watches.

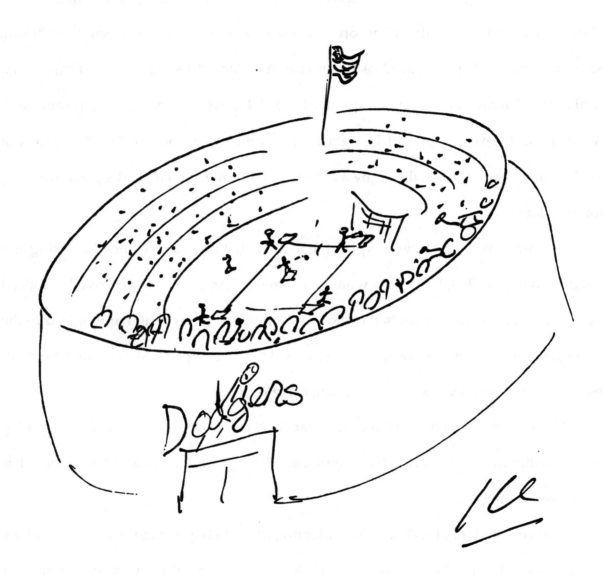

XII.   THE BALL GAME

Vero Beach, Florida is the home of spring training camp for the Los Angeles Dodgers. The ballpark is not far from my home and every spring it's an exciting time at Dodgertown.

We would have liked to have attended some games, but because of Mother's extreme sensitivity to the sun, it wasn't possible. Once, in 1988, Mother was very insistent that my sister and I take my uncle Tom, who was visiting from Ohio, to the ball game. It had to be when Orel Hershiser would be pitching. We did that and we even managed to take a picture of Uncle Tom with Orel Hershiser who was in the middle of a pitch on the mound in the background.

Thirteen years later, the next visit to Dodgertown was with my nephew, Kevin. We were headed to an afternoon ball game. Of course, my mind was focused on how Mom would have loved to be with us. In fact, I said to Kevin, "I wonder if Mom will be with us today at the ball game. At least she doesn't have to worry about her skin."

We got our tickets and on the stubs it said seats Section 9B 5 and 6. We sat down. Both of us looked at each other. There was a penny laying on the floor in front of seat 4. To my astonishment, I said to Kevin, "I guess she is telling us she is with us. How can it be? As large as this stadium is, how does a penny just happen to be in front of seat 4?" Okay, Mom, I guess you finally get to come to a ball game with us.

XIII.   THE PSYCHIATRIST

I could count eight encounters which could not be explained. I fought hard with myself always reflecting that fifty-four years of my life were explainable. A stable environment, a Marine Corps career, a wonderful home life. It was almost too much for anyone to hope for and yet I could claim every moment as being certainly of this earth. Then poof – from fifty-four to fifty-seven years old everything changed. My mother's death changed the whole depth of my life.

Things happened to me now that seem "not to be of this earth." I have always had the privilege of being afforded the services of mental health from the VA, and to avail myself seemed probably the right thing to do. I needed to share the things that were happening to me with a doctor. I knew he would be fair with me. I wondered if they lock people up for stories like mine?

During the first meeting I had with him, I shared what had happened to my friends, Winnie, Hope, and Charlotte. When my mother passed, I would share conversations with each of the three of them. Strangely enough, each of them shared with me, separately, a similar story.

First, Winnie shared with me about how after her husband Johnny died she had been mad at him because he was supposed to take care of her and she felt that he had let her down. Prior to his death, he always took care of her when she had a choking spell. After his death, she had been eating lunch at Morrison's Cafeteria one afternoon and she choked. She became afraid and wondered how Johnny could let something like that

happen to her without him being there to help her. That night, she went to bed and Johnny appeared to her at the foot of his bed. His gray hair and blue plaid shirt stood out. It was as if he was telling her it would be all right now.

Also, Hope shared with me about how her husband Jake had come to her one night at the foot of her bed and seemed to say that he was okay and everything would be all right.

Then, Charlotte explained to me that her husband Earl had come to her at the end of her bed and seemed to let her know that everything would be okay.

How can it be that three ladies, all very spiritual are able to share about the same story of their husbands coming to them after their death to let them know everything will be all right? None of the three were aware of what the other two had shared with me. We are all members of the same church, our Savior Lutheran Church in Vero Beach, Florida.

My friend Marge also shared with me that her mother passed when she was twelve years old. Soon after her mother's death, Marge was laying on the couch and her mother came to her in full view except for her feet and said to her, "You never have to worry about me again, I'm in Heaven."

My mother didn't do this, but as Sylvia Browne revealed in her reading, my mother stroked my cheek while I was sleeping and another time, called out my name. When I was reminded of these things, I had no choice other than to acknowledge that it did happen.

My appointments continued and eventually all of the strange phenomena were relayed to the psychiatrist. I was very comfortable with him and I wanted to know his

MESSAGES FROM: HEAVEN

assessment of what was happening to me. I will always remember what he said to me, "Psychiatry would explain it as hysteria. But I will be as truthful with you as I can." The doctor's father had passed away. He explained that he has experienced moments of his father talking to him after his passing. So, instead of him telling me I was a bit on the crazy side, he only encouraged me that psychiatrists don't have all of the answers and strange things happen to them, too.

I shared with him that I feel my mother has shown me enough that I know she is still with me. I told him I don't think she has to try so hard now, I have the message.

On my way out of the office that day, as I was walking down the hallway, a voice seemed to be saying to me, "I'm really proud of you," as if she knows I can get on with my life now.

I didn't know it at the time, but she was planning at least one more appearance.

XIV.   THE WEDDING

Mother looked at my nephew. She reached for him to lean down to her and when he did, she whispered something in his ear. That took place one day in my sister's yard. Her grandson Kevin was building a shed on his mother's property. I watched as this was taking place and I was very curious as to what was being said. She returned to our car and as she was getting in, I asked her what she was up to. With a sparkle in her eye she said, "I just gave Kevin permission to get married." I will always remember the satisfied look on her face. She was completely confident that this would now occur because she has blessed the moment. She had always before been cautious that marriage at this point may not be the right thing for Kevin. I smiled and asked her if she really thought that now that she thinks it's okay he will listen to his grandmother? Of course he will listen to her. She is the matriarch. All of the family responds to her wishes.

Unfortunately, this took place a couple years before she died and the wedding did not take place in her lifetime. Kevin courted Toni for more than sixteen years and on Mother's Day 2000, my sister was blessed by the news that he was about to get married. Her son chose to tell her by placing the words, "Toni and I are getting married" in small letters on the back of her Mother's Day card. I cannot express the happiness that his old aunt and mother felt at that moment. Extreme happiness. And when it hit me, it took me back to the "whisper in his ear."

The date was set for Saturday, July 8, 2000. The day came and it poured down rain. The wedding was planned to be done outdoors with the reception to follow at Captain

The wedding. Kevin and Toni each keep their special penny.

Hiram's banquet room. However, the weather forced the wedding indoors in the banquet room.

Earlier in the day, I had been with my friend Hope. I commented, "Well, I wonder if Mom will be there for the wedding." Hope smiled and said, "Well, we'll just have to see."

The banquet room was beautifully decorated. The carpeted room is always swept and prepared prior to a function.

The wedding ceremony was performed and all of the guests were served a wonderful dinner. Of course, I felt Mother was with us. She wouldn't miss this for anything. And then I looked down beside my chair. There were two very shiny pennies, both heads up. I leaned down and picked them up. One was 1999 and the other 2000. I said to myself, "Okay, Mom, I knew you would be here." Two pennies – one for Kevin, one for Toni. They were immediately given to Kevin and I told him, "Grandma's here. I found these by my chair." Kevin said, "I'll keep them forever." Two years later when I was visiting him at his home, I asked him if he still had those pennies Grandma dropped at his wedding? He went to the drawer in his room and brought them out for me to see. Like he said, "I'll keep them forever."

XV.   SYLVIA'S READING

The phone rang. It had been more than two years since arrangements had been made to have a psychic reading done by the world-renowned Sylvia Browne. To be on an over two-year wait list, the time had finally come. What can she possibly tell me -- will she know my loss? Will she know what is on my mind? The phone is ringing -- for God's sake -- pick it up! Will it really be Sylvia on the other end of the line -- oh! I recognize her voice! It's really her. What follows is the actual reading which took place on February 28, 2002, when she called my home:

Sylvia: Dian?

Dian: Yes.

Sylvia: This is Sylvia.

Dian: Hi Sylvia.

Sylvia: Listen dear, you know that I'm taping this for us.

Dian: Yes I do.

Sylvia: And the only thing I want you to do is when I'm describing something to you, and I will be very specific, tell me whether it's already happened or not.

Dian: All right.

Sylvia: It doesn't mean that I can't go back in the past, but I'd so much like to get to present and future.

Dian: Okay.

Sylvia: Because I think that's more valid, anyway.

Dian: Oh, it's so nice to hear from you, Sylvia.

Sylvia: Oh, bless your heart. And I'll tell you everything, dear, bad, good, warn you, advise you, but I won't control your life.

Dian: Oh, I know you won't.

Sylvia: Because that's between you and God, honey.

Dian: It's so wonderful to hear from you.

Sylvia: Aw. How are you doing, this sounds really crazy but how are you doing with your depression lately?

Dian: Terrible.

Sylvia: I know you are. We call this loss depressed or grief depressed.

Dian: Yes.

Sylvia: I know this might sound crazy but please try to keep your diet more into the protein because your blood sugar is getting really low.

Dian: Okay.

Sylvia: And that just exacerbates the depression, you see what I mean?

Dian: Okay.

Sylvia: Look, when we're depressed we don't even feel like eating, or if we do, we eat all the wrong things.

Dian: Right. Right.

Sylvia: I'm the same way. Even I can just get goofy on carbohydrates, but see, you can't do that, you're like me, you're an endomorph. You and I have got to stay more

on the protein.

Dian: Okay.

Sylvia: That's why you get so tired about 10:00, 4:00, and 6:00. You see what I'm saying?

You get draggy. And that's because your protein's not holding.

Dian: Thank you very much.

Sylvia: Uh huh. And you're like me. You hate to be tired. See you've always been an

up-and-at-em girl. See your primary theme is activator, your secondary theme is

humanitarian, so there's nothing in those two themes that want you to be tired

and dragging around and feeling yuk.

Dian: Okay.

Sylvia: Now, what is all this writing you're doing?

Dian: Ah, I'm writing a book.

Sylvia: But that's a good thing.

Dian: You know my loss, right?

Sylvia: Your mom.

Dian: Yes.

Sylvia: You know, she comes around you a lot.

Dian: I've been told that.

Sylvia: Ah, did she have an oval face, beautiful eyes, straight nose, pretty skin, wore hair

either short or back?

Dian: Oh yes.

Sylvia: Well that's her.

Dian: Red hair?

Sylvia: Un huh. And not because she had red hair but, very stubborn.

Dian: Oh yes. Absolutely.

Sylvia: She says she's come around you in three dreams. She sat on your bed one night. And she also comes around with a scent.

Dian: In her bedroom.

Sylvia: Yes. You know you walk in, you say, oh, that's a floral scent.

Dian: Yes.

Sylvia: I don't know what this means . . . she said she heard you talking to her before she passed.

Dian: Yes.

Sylvia: But she sure fought, honey. And then she did finally give up.

Dian: Yes.

Sylvia: But we're talking about a strong woman. We're talking about also a very spiritual, good woman.

Dian: Oh yes.

Sylvia: You know, not to be brag on us, but we're kind of like the dying dinosaurs, you know they don't make women like us anymore, I mean real women, you know what I mean. Today they're kind of "help me, hold me, take care of me" women.

We don't come from that genre.

Dian: No.

Sylvia: And when we go I think that's the end of it, you know what I mean?

Dian: Yes. Sylvia, I'm very depressed over the loss of my mom.

Sylvia: I know.

Dian: I want to listen to you before I ask any questions.

Sylvia: She keeps talking about rings, what does that mean, rings?

Dian: Rings.

Sylvia: Yes.

Dian: Her silver rings, that's part of my book

Sylvia: Yes.

Dian: They went away for a while.

Sylvia: Yes.

Dian: And that's part of my book, that all of a sudden the ring box came back.

Sylvia: Uh huh. That's what we call aport in my business.

Dian: Well, they were gone for awhile and then I found them right in front of my eyes.

Sylvia: Well, she placed them there, honey.

Dian: She took them and then she put them back.

Sylvia: Uh huh. That's what we call aport.

Dian: I knew it. And that's why I'm writing a book, Sylvia, it's called *God, Mom, and Me.*

Sylvia: Yes. You know, remember in *Reader's Digest* "The Most Unforgettable Character"

-- you remember that excerpt -- that's what this reminds me of except elongated and much more specific.

Dian: Okay.

Sylvia: You know, telling about her life, your life interwoven, and your spiritual journey.

Dian: Yes.

Sylvia: Uh huh. And God, that'll make it. Do you know what I mean? I'm not just talking about writing for fun and games, I'm talking about writing for publication.

Dian: Well.....

Sylvia: Because see, what you've got to realize, you could sit down with paper at hand, or whatever, and you're going to get a lot of infusion, you know what I mean? You write, you think, God that's good. She's helping you infuse. It's very much like not just automatic writing, automatic thinking writing.

Dian: Does she do that when I cook?

Sylvia: Yeah. Everything.

Dian: And she's okay?

Sylvia: Oh, honey, she made it like a shotgun. I mean she was this, boom.

Dian: You know what, that's the second time I was told that, she was there in a minute.

Sylvia: Oh, God, honey, it's been a long time since I saw anybody shoot that fast. I mean usually they kind of dawdle around. Now what does she keep talking about two, two services, what does that mean? Two services.

Dian: I don't know.

Sylvia: She said there was a memorial service and then a small gathering of some kind.

Dian: Oh yes. At the church and then we had one at Hillcrest Memorial Gardens.

Sylvia: Yes. That's what she means. She said two services, like, two.

Dian: Did she like that?

Sylvia: She loved it.

Dian: That's wonderful.

Sylvia: Now what's the picture with the candle?

Dian: Picture with a candle.

Sylvia: Uh huh.

Dian: I'm not sure. I don't know right now.

Sylvia: She said there's a picture that you have of you and she. And then there's a candle. I don't know what that means. Maybe she wants you to light a candle, I don't know, but she keeps talking about a candle. (I didn't realize it at the time, but our picture sits on the counter in the kitchen and a candle sits beside it.)

Dian: Ooh, this is marvelous.

Sylvia: She said one night when you were sleeping on your side, she put a hand on your face. It was feathery feeling, you know, like you felt that there was a presence.

Dian: Yes, I did.

Sylvia: Uh huh. She said she also called your name out one morning.

Dian: I'm sure.

Sylvia: You know how you bolt up and think, oh I was sleeping or I was dreaming?

Dian: Yes.

Sylvia: No. That was her, honey.

Dian: Ah.

Sylvia: Now, who's Ann? Or Anna?

Dian: I don't know.

Sylvia: She's with an Ann.

Dian: I don't know, I was hoping that you'd tell me that. Aunt Barbara passed away too.

Sylvia: Oh Barbara's there but she said please check on Ann because I think that validates that she would know something you would know.

Dian: Ann does not ring a bell with me at all.

Sylvia: Well, of course there's not many people to ask, but I think you'll run across her because it's from her side of the family way back.

Dian: Okay.

Sylvia: Yes. I had somebody, honey, show up around me by the name of Lena, and I had to go to the old family Bible and find out it was a great-grandmother.

Dian: Oh, may I start asking questions?

Sylvia: Sure, you can ask anything.

Dian: All right.

Sylvia: What is this, it sounds so crazy, what is this military stuff?

Dian: I was in the military for many years.

Sylvia: Oh, well that's probably what it is. She won't shut up so I'm not going to shut her up.

Dian: Okay.

Sylvia: She says she's glad you're out of that because she always worried.

Dian: Yes.

Sylvia: Well, I think that's as a mother. But she was excessively worried.

Dian: Yes, I was a Marine for 15 years.

Sylvia: Yes, she was always afraid you were going to get blown up, hurt, or shot.

Dian: That would have been all right.

Sylvia: Absolutely. Well thank goodness it's your last life.

Dian: It's my last life? Thank God.

Sylvia: Isn't that the truth.

Dian: Have I learned to be humble and forgive?

Sylvia: Yes. Well it's not so much that, you just passed your tests.

Dian: Okay.

Phones disconnected, reconnected.

Dian: Hello?

Sylvia: Yes, I don't know what happened, the phone just went dead.

Dian: Mine too.

Sylvia: Yeah, it just went boop.

Dian: Yes. Sylvia, she seems to drop coins.

Sylvia: Coins dropping. I don't know why that is but I began to pick it up about, oh, maybe 15 years ago. They really drop coins. Something else they do, which she does, is make birds appear.

Dian: Okay.

Sylvia: You know you'll see, well I mean everybody has birds, but all of a sudden you have a bird there. And then there's another bird there. And then another bird.

Dian: Yes. Okay. Um, Sylvia, I have a great emptiness. Is there anything you can tell me . . .

Sylvia: Oh honey, you know something. I lost nine people in three months. My dad, my mother, everybody. Ah, you know, if only there was a pill. It's like one day at a time, but I do know this because she's so happy and she's still around you and by June you start feeling this shroud, so to speak, lift.

Dian: Oh.

Sylvia: But there's no easy way to do this.

Dian: Right.

Sylvia: If I knew an easy way I'd tell you. There wasn't an easy way for me. See, what we're caught is in a conundrum. It's like we're happy for them but we miss them. Yes, it's the double-edged sword.

Dian: Oh yes.

Sylvia: And I hate to tell you this, but like I said you have a long life, but see, to her it's like a few days.

Dian: We'll be together again?

Sylvia: Oh God, honey, you're soul mates. A soul mate can be anybody. It can be your mother, it can be your granddaughter, your sister, it could be your husband, but I mean so many times I've seen even friend soul mates.

Dian: Yes.

Dian: You know, my mom was my soul mate.

Sylvia: Absolutely.

Dian: Yes. Here's my question, okay?

Sylvia: All right.

Dian: Was there a man in heaven waiting for my mom?

Sylvia: Yes. An older man.

Dian: Oh.

Sylvia: Stocky build.

Dian: Yes. My step-dad.

Sylvia: Broad face.

Dian: Yes.

Sylvia: Receding hairline.

Dian: Yes.

Sylvia: Yes, he was there.

Dian: My step-dad, Tom.

Sylvia: Yes.

Dian: Was Mom met by anyone prior to going to heaven?

Sylvia: Well, her guide was there.

Dian: Okay.

Sylvia: Rebecca was there, but also there was a little woman, short, small.

Dian: My Aunt Bea.

Sylvia: Pardon me?

Dian: My Aunt Bea.

Sylvia: Yes, small woman.

Dian: I was told previously that she was met by her sister. Okay. My dog, Kermit died on Valentine's Day. I'm wondering if he's with her.

Sylvia: She's got two dogs over there. There's a medium sized one and a large one.

Dian: Ah. Black and white, maybe?

Sylvia: Yes. Absolutely.

Dian: Well, he just died on Valentine's Day.

Sylvia: Well, she got him. Remember when I said she's working with the animals, gardening, helping people in and out.

Dian: Okay. All right. Did she come back as her great grandbaby, Emily?

Sylvia: No honey. She not gonna come back. She's waiting for you. She's not coming back.

Sylvia: She's not coming back.

91

Dian: Okay.

Sylvia: I don't think somebody could beg, borrow, or steal, you know, no, she's not coming back. She was waiting for you.

Dian: Okay. Will my nephew Kevin and his wife Toni, have any more children?

Sylvia: A girl.

Dian: A girl?

Sylvia: Uh huh.

Dian: Another girl?

Sylvia: Another girl.

Dian: I guess twins are not possible, right?

Sylvia: No. Not in this life.

Dian: All right. Are there any health issues life-threatening for my nephew?

Sylvia: No. No. I mean we're talking about a little cold, a little high-strung, but that's not a health issue.

Dian: Okay. My sister lost some store money a few years ago and has no idea what happened to it. Do you have any feelings about that?

Sylvia: Honey, she lost it.

Dian: She lost it.

Sylvia: She lost it. It wasn't taken. She lost it.

Dian: She lost it.

Sylvia: I don't mean she took it, she lost it.

Dian: Oh, well Sylvia, I don't want to hold you. I know you are a busy lady -- you have

          answered all of my questions and I do think I am going to start to heal now.

Sylvia: You will, honey, I know you will because your mom is waiting for you. My dad's

          waiting for me. We all be up there and have a party.

Dian: Oh, we will.

Sylvia: I know we will.

Dian: All right.

Sylvia: All right, darling.

Dian: Thank you very much. Goodbye.

Girl's hunt for penny
comes up with
1.5 carat diamond

XVI.   FRONT PAGE NEWS

Friday night, May 2, 2002, I really felt very satisfied knowing that I have managed to document all but two of the incidents. The ball game and the wedding are the two that I would need to finish. Both of them deal with pennies.

After breakfast on Saturday morning, May 3, 2002, I picked up the Vero Beach *Press Journal* newspaper and noticed a headline: "Girl's hunt for Penny Comes up with 1.5 carat diamond." I chuckled to myself because for many years I have always said, "If God wanted me to bend over, he would have put diamonds on the floor." I believe I heard Joan Rivers say it and it has stuck with me. As I read the article, I had no idea what it would contain. It was hardly "just" finding a diamond. With reprint permission from the *Jupiter Courier*, the article follows:

Girl's Hunt for Penny Comes Up with 1.5 Carat Diamond

When 7-year-old Carli Homish discovered a 1.5 carat diamond on the floor of Jupiter's new T.J. Maxx last month, she also found a "penny from heaven."

Carli was looking down as she walked with her mother toward the checkout line at T.J. Maxx in Concourse Village at Indiantown Road and Alternate A1A. A sparkle on the tile floor caught her eye.

The first-grader picked up the bright rock and handed it to her mother.

"Carli's always picking things up," Patty Homish said. "When she handed it to me at first, I thought it was a screw."

The diamond, which police said has an estimated replacement value of $6,000, was nestled in a six-prong setting that had broken off a ring.

While Carli waited at the customer service counter for her mother to turn in the diamond, Carli also discovered a shiny 2002 penny at her feet.

"I always look at the floor," Carli said. "I don't pick up my head."

For the diamond's owner, part-time Jupiter resident Nancy Plunkett, Carli's discovery of the penny – was a message from above.

Larry and Nancy Plunkett lost their 16-year-old son Eric in a traffic accident in Missouri in 1985. Before he died, the teen told his mother that whenever she found a penny, she should think of him.

As Mrs. Plunkett raced back to T.J. Maxx to find her diamond, she too, found a penny at the customer service desk.

"I looked up at the sky and said 'OK, Eric, this is in your hands,'" Mrs. Plunkett said.

She said she knew the angels were at work. "He was always crazy about pennies, so this became my 'penny connection' to Eric," she said.

Mrs. Plunkett had been shopping the morning of April 7, grand opening day for T.J. Maxx.

"I was looking for a mate for a quilt," she said Friday from her summer home outside St. Louis. While she was shopping, the diamond, still clasped in the prongs, broke off.

"Later that morning, we were heading off for a late breakfast when my husband noticed the stone was gone," she recalled.

When Carli found the diamond three days later, T.J. Maxx managers told Mrs. Homish that a woman had reported losing a stone. The managers recorded the Homishes' phone number and turned the diamond over to Jupiter police, who called the Plunketts with the good news.

That night, a grateful Mrs. Plunkett called Mrs. Homish to thank her for the return of the gem, a gift years ago from her husband.

The two families made plans to meet the next day. Carli, still clutching her penny, asked her mother: "Do you think she'll give me candy?"

The Plunketts and Patty and Carli Homish met in front of Albertsons supermarket near Jonathan's Landing. Mrs. Plunkett gave thank-you cards to the mother and daughter, along with a $200 reward for Carli. Carli gave Nancy Plunkett her penny.

When Nancy Plunkett shared her "penny story," there wasn't a dry eye to be found.

In searching for an appropriate card for Carli, Nancy Plunkett said: "I looked at six cards and none was right. I moved down the aisle, then came back and there was a seventh card right there; it was *not* there before, and it had two angels on it."

The card read: "I guess your guardian angel and my guardian angel shop together."

Wrote Plunkett: "Do you think we have guardian angels watching over us? There is no way I can thank you for being such a wonderful young lady. When things go wrong in this world I won't feel so bad, because with people like you around it gives me hope."

"This was such a wonderful, touching and emotional feeling for me," Mrs. Plunkett said. "And Carli is just the sweetest little girl. What a wonderful family."

~ ~ ~ ~ ~ ~ ~ ~

Isn't that interesting? I felt compelled to contact Nancy Plunkett to talk with her – from 1985 to 2002. Time doesn't really matter.

I made every effort to contact Mrs. Plunkett. The article said she returned to St. Louis. I went on an all-out search. All I could hope for after I exhausted all efforts which include unlisted phone numbers, a police report with no case number, Dixie at T.J. Maxx unable to locate any information, and the staff writer, Randall Murray, at the *Press Journal* helping me by leaving a message for her at a cell phone number – I had to wait.

On May 7, 2002, I received a phone call. My caller ID said from Missouri. Before I picked it up, I knew it was from Nancy Plunkett. We shared a very intriguing conversation. She told me how her story was told by Paul Harvey in his broadcast. She shared with me about the loss of her son. We both agreed about how we try to see so hard about what is behind the curtain. And most of all, we agreed that we want to share our stories to give others hope because of our truly remarkable experiences. Also, we both realize that this doesn't happen to everyone. You truly have to be open to receive the messages from Heaven. What we shared together is confirmation that these experiences really do take place. We also found that we are both 57 years old and we are members of the Lutheran Church. I thought about that – six Lutheran women all experiencing "strange" phenomena. I really think it has more to do with the deep love we share in the loss of our loved ones and a very deep spiritual connection. I am certain our experiences are only the tip of the iceberg and many people from all denominations have things happen to them that haven't been documented or freely shared with others.

XVII.   FATHER LIEFFORT

On December 6, 2001, I attended a Remembrance Service in honor of our loved ones who are no longer with us. I have attended each year since 1999. There is always representation from all faiths and each of the clergymen speak. This year in particular, one of the clergymen, Father Lieffort from St. Sebastian by the Sea Episcopal Church in Palm Bay, Florida offered such a beautiful tribute which I just knew needed to be part of this book. With his permission, his words are shared with you:

My dear brothers and sisters,

Tonight we gather to celebrate life . . . The lives of those who have gone on before us to the greater life to come . . . those whose lives have touched us by the quality of their caring, and given us a reminder of how fragile and precious life is. We also come together to mourn for ourselves . . . for the separation we feel . . . for the deepest hurt of our hearts . . . not being able to touch, to hear, to see, except in our soul's eye.

Those of you who have children or grandchildren know that a few years ago, Walt Disney put out a movie entitled "Lion King." One of the featured songs was "The Circle of Life." Long before Elton John recorded that song, the Bible taught us of the circle of life. A folk singer 30 years ago sang a paraphrase of one of the sections of wisdom literature in the Bible and reminded us, "To everything *turn, turn, turn*, there is a season *turn, turn, turn*, and a time for every purpose under heaven."

My father died a few years ago at the ripe old age of 86. The last few months of his life were very painful and frustrating for him. Hospice volunteers ministered to him in their own wonderful way. One day he said to me, "Bob, all my hair is gone. I'm bald, I'm wrinkled, I don't have teeth, and I'm wearing diapers. God must be recycling me, because I'm leaving this world just like I came into it . . . I'm a baby again!"

One of the earliest symbols of the life to come was the butterfly, carved into the coffins of the early martyrs. Butterflies don't start out that way . . . they begin as caterpillars. They live a rather bland existence, creeping along branches and leaves, subject to many dangers, but one day, ready or not, they have to shed their old skin. In that painful process, the only thing they know for sure is that they are dying. Yet in just a few hours they are transformed. They have wings with which to soar above the clouds. They live in the same world, yet they have a whole new panorama and freedom about them.

If we could ask them if they were willing to be a caterpillar again, they would explain to us that as long as that was all they knew, it was fine. But now that they had been a butterfly, they could never be happy as a caterpillar again. Doctors tell us that all of us have had a similar experience. It was so painful and traumatic that we have suppressed it in the recesses of our memories.

Once life was nearly perfect for us . . . we were insulated from loud noise and from bright lights, we spent our days in perfect contentment, just floating in nice warm water. We didn't even have to feed ourselves, that was done for us through our belly buttons. One day, however, all that changed. Ready or not, we were propelled down the birth canal. For the first time, we experienced pain as the contracting muscles around us crushed down on us and slowly moved us down the tunnel toward the light . . . sound familiar? In that moment of sheer terror, all we knew for sure is that we were dying. All the stories we read about life after life experience use the same phrase . . . down the tunnel toward the light. Wouldn't it have been wonderful if some doctor or nurse could have assured us that we were not dying . . . that we had not even lived yet . . . we were just being born.

I believe in the circle of life. One day we shall be transformed. Only this time at that very moment when all we know is that we are dying, we shall hear God's voice calling us tenderly and assuring us that we need not be afraid . . . we're just being born . . . we haven't even lived yet. Instead of being delivered into the hands of a doctor, we shall wake to new and eternal life in the arms of Our Lord.

Amen.

I hope what I have shared with you gives you insight and encouragement that our loved ones who have passed remain with us. Someone once said, a person only dies when there is no longer anyone to remember them.

The End

P.S. Sylvia was right! It's a girl!

‖‖ ‖ ‖‖‖‖ ‖‖ ‖‖‖‖‖‖‖‖ ‖ ‖‖‖‖‖‖‖‖‖‖ ‖ ‖‖ ‖ ‖‖ ‖‖

Printed in the United States
By Bookmasters